TOTALLY STUPID MEN

TOTALLY STUPID MEN

Hysterical home truths about the men in your life

Michael O'Mara Books Limited

First published in Great Britain in 1997 by
Michael O'Mara Books Limited
9 Lion Yard
Tremadoc Road
London SW4 7NQ

A CIP catalogue record for this book is available from the British Library

ISBN 1-85479-265-2

1 3 5 7 9 10 8 6 4 2

Designed by Mick Keates
Typeset by Concise Artisans

Printed and bound in Finland by WSOY

CONTENTS

YOU'RE SO STUPID

What do you call a fisherman?

*A jerk on one line waiting for
a jerk on the other.*

**Why don't women work as long
and hard as men in the office?**

They do it right the first time.

**Why are male brains considered
a better donation to science?**

They haven't been used.

**How can you recognise a
stupid man's pencil?**

It has a rubber at both ends.

A man's first experience of life is trying to get out of a woman's body and then he spends the rest of his life trying to get back in.

I hate men who...

talk out of the back of their heads

Why are men like bank accounts?

One day they're up,
the next they're down,
and most of the time
they show no interest.

My husband is so sensitive
about his hair.
I don't know why...
he hasn't got any.

Man:
**What would you say if
I asked you to marry me?**

Woman:
**Nothing, I can't laugh
and talk at the same time.**

**Did you hear about the guy
who was so stupid he had to
drop his trousers to count to 21?**

**Why do men complain women
have no sense of humour when
they have no sense and
even less humour?**

**More husbands would leave home
if they knew how to pack.**

**How does a stupid man make
sex more interesting?**

He leaves town.

One girlfriend said
to another girlfriend,
'My most secret fantasy is
having two men at once.'

'Really, why?' asked the other.

'One for cooking, the other
for cleaning.'

My husband is a self-made man
and he worships his creator.

Two stupid workmen were digging
out a quarry with a gigantic excavator.
One said to the other, 'It's a crying
shame; this quarry would provide work
for a thousand men with shovels.'

The other replied, 'Or a million men
with teaspoons.'

I hate men who...

say, 'trust me!'

**What three little words
will you never hear
a stupid man say?**

It's on me.

**How can you recognise
a stupid man's helicopter?**

It has an ejection seat.

Why did the stupid man go parachuting?

Who knows why he does anything?

How does a stupid man cook dinner?

I don't know, he's never done it.

Why do stupid men think they're so clever?

Who cares?

How do you spot a stupid pirate?

He has a patch over both eyes.

Down at the pub one stupid
man was talking to another:
'What has six balls and
screws you twice a week?'

'I dunno know, what?'
slurped the other.

'The Lottery.'

When the stupid man says he takes life with a pinch of salt, it's true... it's just that he takes it with a slice of lemon and a shot of tequila, too.

A man marries a woman hoping she'll never change and a woman marries a man hoping he will.

**What is the first prize in the
stupid man's lottery?**

£10 a year for a million years.

**What do people say when a
stupid man enters a room with a
beautiful woman on his arm?**

'Where did you get the tattoo?'

Men don't get excited about women's minds, they get excited about what they don't mind.

What does it mean to come home to a man who'll give you some love and tenderness?

You're in the wrong house.

**How do dumb men define
a sharing relationship?**

They eat – we cook.

Wife:
**Who was that woman I saw
kissing you last night?**

Husband:
What time was it?

I hate men who...

pick their teeth

**Why is a stupid man like
a microwave?**

Thirty seconds and he's finished.

Why do men act like idiots?

Who says they're acting?

**How do you find out what
life is like without
a man around?**

Get married.

**What's the difference between
an intelligent man and
a stupid man?**

*Nothing, they both think
they know everything.*

Why doesn't a stupid man believe in the new Messiah?

Because to him a second coming is an impossibility.

Did you hear about the man who makes love like he drives his car?

He goes too fast and gets there before anyone else.

How can you tell if a man is lying?

His lips are moving.

Why are all the dumb blonde jokes one-liners?

So men can understand them.

Husband:
Let's go out and have some fun tonight.

Wife:
Okay, but if you get home before I do, just remember to leave the front door open.

A man came home and found his
wife in bed with his best friend.
'What are you doing?'
he shouted.

'See?' she said to her lover.
'Didn't I tell you he was stupid?'

**You don't need to lead a man
into temptation – he can usually
find it on his own.**

**What do you call a man
who tidies up after himself?**

An over-achiever.

**Not all women are silly –
some are single.**

**Why is a man like a
food processor?**

*You know you need one
but you're not quite sure why.*

What's the best way to keep a stupid man happy in the bedroom?

Put the TV in the bedroom and turn on the football.

How do you keep a stupid man from wanting sex?

Marry him.

I hate men who...

leave the seat up
(among other things)

**Why did the stupid man
throw away his toilet brush?**

He discovered toilet paper.

**What are the ups and
down of marriage?**

*The toilet seat is always up
and his interest is always down.*

Plumber:
Where's the drip?

Wife:
**He's in the bathroom trying
to fix the leak.**

**How do you keep a stupid man
from wanting the other woman?**

Divorce him.

**How do you lose
fourteen stone of fat?**

Divorce him.

**What does a stupid man do
when confronted by a toddler
having a tantrum?**

Stamps his feet and shouts for mother.

**What do you call a stupid man
who uses the rhythm method?**

Dad.

**What's the definition of a
well-informed man?**

Someone who agrees with you.

**How many men does it take
to milk a cow?**

**Twenty-four; one on each teat and
twenty to lift the cow up and down.**

**A woman, at any age, likes
a man with a will of his own –
made out in her favour
of course.**

**How does a stupid man
count money?**

1,2,3,4,5, another, another, another…

How do we know Adam was stupid?

Would a clever man eat an apple when a naked woman was discussing temptation?

Love, companionship and sex
are the three things a
woman needs from a man.
By the time a woman comes
of age she knows she will
have to go to three different
places for it.

The science teacher came in
and addressed one of her students:
'Can you tell me which portion
of the human anatomy swells
ten times its normal size
during periods of agitation
or emotional excitement?'

Blushing, the shy girl stammered,
'I-I would rather n-not answer
that q-question.'

Arching a brow the teacher asked,
'Oh? And why not?'

'Well, it's too embarrassing to say.'
said the student.

'Not at all!' huffed the teacher,
'The correct answer is the
pupil of the eyes, and your
response tells me two things:
first, that you didn't read
last night's homework and
second that marriage is going
to leave you a tremendously
disappointed young woman.'

I hate men who...

swirl drinks with their fingers

**Women at forty are
at their best, but men of forty
are too stupid to realise it.**

**What's the best way to
get a man to remember
your anniversary?**

Get married on his birthday.

Is an IQ of 180 considered high?

*No, not when you consider
it's the total IQ of eight men.*

How is a stupid man
like a python?

*No sane person would go to bed
with either of them.*

After struggling to open his
beer the man leaned over
to the cocktail waitress:
'Excuse me, I was wondering
if you could help me out?'

'Certainly,' smiled the waitress,
'go right through that door.'

'Yes,' said the man to his barber,
'split hair is a problem.
Mine split about five years ago.'

**How did the stupid man
die drinking milk?**

The cow fell on him.

Husband to wife:
'Honey, do you think these
trousers need altering, are they
too big on me?'

'No, they don't need altering,
but you do.'

**How many stupid men
does it take to change the
toilet paper roll?**

Don't know, it's never happened before.

**How do you know a fax is
from a stupid man?**

There's a stamp on it.

**Wife to her husband:
'Honey, why don't you take up
jogging again? It's the only time
I ever get to hear your
heavy breathing.'**

'Perhaps,' suggested the
shop assistant, 'your wife might
like some cucumber soap
for her birthday?'

'I don't think so,' he replied,
'she just rinses them
off with water.'

The husband walked over to the perfume counter and told the shop assistant he'd like a bottle of Chanel No.5 for his wife's birthday.

'A little surprise?' smiled the clerk.

'You bet,' answered the husband, 'she's expecting an all-expenses-paid trip to New York.'

What's a stupid man's idea of a varied diet?

A quarter-pounder with cheese one day and without cheese the next.

Why don't stupid men's dogs do tricks?

You have to be more intelligent than a dog to teach it tricks.

My husband takes the biscuit. Whenever we go to a new hotel room, he insists on taking home the soap and shampoo from the bathroom. One night I caught him walking down the hall trick-or-treating.

No, my husband takes the biscuit.
We bought these new car
phones that give you thirty
minutes of free call time on the
weekends. I went down to the
garage to look for my husband.
He was sitting in the car talking
to his best friend with an egg
timer on the dashboard.

A man walks into the chemist,
'Can I buy some male protection?'
he enquires. 'How much does it cost?'

'That'll be £5.00 including tax.'
said the shopkeeper.

'Ah,' said the man, 'I always wondered
how you keep them up.'

I hate men who...

ogle

The bookshop assistant was talking to his new trainee: 'Did you see that new book *50 Ways to Mate*, translated from Russian with 100 illustrations, it's practically running out of the shop...
I've never seen a book on chess sell so well.'

Wife to her husband:
'Honey, why are you home so early?'

'Well, I'm so mad – I had a fight
with my boss and he wouldn't
take back what he said.'

'What did he say?' said
the shocked wife.

'You're fired!'

**Why did the stupid man buy
an electric lawnmower?**

*So he could find his way
back to the house.*

**How are men like dogs
about housework?**

*They run and hide every time
they see a vacuum cleaner.*

I hate men who...

spread out on public transport

A woman went into the pet shop
to confront the owner, Barney:
'I want to return this cat. You said
it was good for mice, but all it
does is lie there.'

'So,' he replied, 'isn't that
good for mice?'

**Why do stupid men write T.G.I.F.
on their shoes?**

To tell them: 'Toes go in first.'

**How can you tell if a stupid man
is cheating on you?**

*He has a bath more than
once a month.*

**'Do you think you could fall for me?'
asked the man at the bar.**

'Only if you pushed me.'

Why do stupid men drive BMWs?

Because they can spell it.

What's the difference between a man and a shopping trolley?

A shopping trolley has a mind of its own.

Why did the stupid man get a stabbing pain in his eye every time he drank a cup of tea?

He forgot to take the spoon out.

**What do you call a stupid man
with headphones on?**

Anything you like, he can't hear you.

**What do you see when you
look into a stupid man's eyes?**

The back of his head.

I hate men who...

wear mirrored sunglasses

An Englishman, a Scotsman and
an Irishman were all sentenced
to death by firing squad.
The Englishman was brought
out first and the firing squad
took aim, when suddenly the
Englishman yelled out, 'AVALANCHE!'
In the confusion that followed
he escaped. Next the Scotsman
thought he would try something
similar. As the firing squad took
aim he yelled, 'FLOOD!', and he too
made his escape. Finally, it was
the Irishman's turn. Confident
of following in his friends' footsteps,
as the firing squad took aim,
he yelled, 'FIRE!'

How do you confuse a stupid man?

You don't, they're born that way.

When I asked my fiancé this morning why his coffee tasted like mud, he said that's perfectly natural, honey, after all it was only ground this morning.

What's black and fuzzy and hangs from the ceiling?

A stupid electrician.

In a room full of interesting people what is the only thing a stupid man sees?

The bimbo and his rival.

'I'd like to be included in
your next edition.' said the guy
on the phone to the
Guinness Book of Records.

'Why, what have you done?'
came the reply.

'I've completed a paint-by-number
in just under a week and
on the box it said
three to five years.'

A woman and her stupid husband
were having a tea party.
'Put out the sugar tongs,' she told him.
'Otherwise your filthy friends
will go to the loo, pee all over their
fingers and then handle the sugar
cubes.' After the party the
wife complained that the sugar tongs
weren't on the table.

'On the table?' her husband cried.
'I put them in the toilet!'

I hate men who…

never use deodorant

A wife yelled at her husband when he came home late from work again, 'You should've been here at 6 o'clock!'

He replied, 'Why, what happened?'

How do you know when your boyfriend is really stupid?

When he knows what he wants but he can't spell it.

'Doctor, doctor, I have
a real problem down under.
I keep thinking I'm
getting smaller.'

'Why? I can't see anything
down there.'

**How many men does it take
to change a lightbulb?**

*Ten – one to put it in and nine
to congratulate him down the pub.*

**When do men insist that
women are illogical?**

*When a woman doesn't
agree with them.*

**Why does a stupid man have
a hole in his pocket?**

So he can count to six.

**My husband says he has
a wonderful personality...
he's obviously saving it
for a special occasion.**

Did you hear about the
family who sent their son
to summer camp?

The boy wrote home he
had grown another foot
so his father knitted
him another sock.

You can't change a man...
even if you could, the only
person who would appreciate
it is his next wife.

Two men were passengers on
a four-engine plane. Suddenly one
engine failed and the pilot announced
that the plane would now be fifteen
minutes late. A short time later another
engine failed. The pilot announced
they would be thirty minutes late.
Then the third engine failed and the
pilot announced that they would be
one hour late.
At this point one man said
to the other, 'If the fourth engine
quits we could be up here all day.'

While driving through the
back roads, two stupid lorry
drivers came to a bridge
with a sign on it that read,
'CLEARANCE 11' 3'''.

They got out and measured
the lorry and it was 12' 4" tall.

'What do you think?'
said one to the other.

The driver looked around
and replied, 'Not a policeman
in sight. Let's take a chance.'

**What's the difference between
a baby and your husband?**

*You can leave a baby alone
with the babysitter.*

**What quality do most men
look for in a woman?**

Breathing.

I hate men who . . .

wear sandals and socks

Where's the safest place to hide money from your husband?

Under the soap.

How do you brainwash a man?

Step on his enema bag.

**Did you hear about
the stupid man
who thought he was
a half-breed?**

*His father was a man and
his mother was a woman.*

**What is special about
a stupid man's parachute?**

It opens on impact.

A woman came into the
police station to report
her husband missing and
described him as '29 years old,
6 feet 3 inches tall, blonde
and handsome.'

'I knew your husband.'
said the desk sergeant.
'He was bald, fat and forty.'

'I know,' the woman replied,
'but who wants HIM back?'

A man was visiting his
barber and as a special treat
the barber pulled out his
new home brew of hair tonic
to use on his customer.

'Hey, don't do that,'
shouted the customer,
'my wife will think I smell
like a brothel.'

Another customer who was
eavesdropping jumped in,
'I don't mind, when it's my
turn you can load me up on
the stuff – my wife doesn't
know what a brothel
smells like.'

In the sports shop a golfer
was talking to the shop owner.
'You know, it isn't such a good
deal to get my golf balls here
anymore. I can go to New York
and get a whole box for
five dollars.'

'Yeah,' said the owner,
'but what about the airfare?'

Did you hear about the man who didn't know which way the lift was going even though they gave him two guesses?

Did you hear about the farmer who ran a steamroller across his fields because he wanted to market mashed potatoes?

A guy shows up at his
date's apartment soaking wet.
When she opens the door she
can't believe her eyes:
'Why is your shirt dripping
with water?' she exclaims.

'Well, the label said
"Wash-n-Wear",' he replies.

I hate men who...

wipe cutlery on the tablecloth

**Why did the stupid man lose
his job as a lift attendant?**

He couldn't learn the route.

**After being married for years,
one night a couple were making
love and the husband asked
'I didn't hurt you, darling, did I?'**

'No,' she replied, 'why do you ask?'

'You moved.'

A handyman was invited into a
wealthy businessman's home
to build some shelves in his library.
'That's a nice moosehead you've
got on the wall. Any chance I can go
into the next room and see the
rest of it?'

Why couldn't the stupid man
make ice cubes?

He lost the recipe.

**Did you hear about the stupid
newly-wed who didn't know
the difference between Vaseline
and putty?**

His windows fell out.

**Why did the stupid newly-wed
stay up all night?**

He was waiting for his sexual relations.

**What's the only time a
man thinks about
a candlelight dinner?**

When the power goes off.

**What did God say
after he created Eve?**

Practice makes perfect.

How are men like carpet tiles?

If you lay them properly the first time around, you can walk all over them for the rest of your life.

Why does a man only get half-hour lunch-breaks?

So his boss doesn't have to retrain him.

What one thing did God do right when he created man?

He created woman to explain the difference between his black and navy blue socks.

There was a man so stupid he didn't know arson from incest.

He set his sister on fire.

I hate men who...

disappear into the loo for hours at a time

How does a stupid man know dinner is ready?

The smoke alarm goes off.

How did the wife stop her stupid husband biting his nails?

She made him wear shoes.

**What is the best birth-control
device for a stupid man?**

His face.

**Did you hear about
the man who was raking up
leaves in his garden?**

He fell out of the tree.

**What's the useless piece
of skin attached to the
male member?**

A man.

**Why do so few men
end up in Heaven?**

They never stop to ask directions.

**What's the only exercise
men are good at?**

*Sucking in their stomachs
every time they see a bikini.*

**I wouldn't say he's handsome.
I wouldn't, but he would.**

How do stupid people reproduce?

They exchange underwear.

What does a stupid man say when he proposes marriage?

'You are going to have a WHAT?'

One girlfriend to another:
It seems that common sense would prevent a lot divorces.

The other:
Yes, and a lot of marriages, too.

'Mummy,' said the stupid boy,
'I have the biggest willie
in the third form. Is it because
I'm advanced?'

'No,' said mother,
'it's because you're fifteen.'

Why did the stupid man put his willie in boiling water?

His wife told him to get sterilised.

How do you make a stupid man's eyes twinkle?

Shine a torch in his ear.

'Daddy, can you make
a noise like a frog?' asked
the stupid man's son.

'Why do you ask that?'
said his father.

'Because Mummy said that
she'll be glad when you croak.'

**The great thing about being
a stupid man is you can
hide your own Easter egg.**

**What do we women have to do...
paint a bull's eye in the
toilet bowl in order to get him
to aim it in there?**

'Mummy, what happens when a car gets too old and rusty to work?' the little girl asked.

'Well,' her mother said, 'someone sells it to your father.'

What do you call a man who supports a woman's career, helps prepare dinner, bathes the kids, and earns a six-figure income?

Darling.

'Am I your first?' asked the Latin lover after sex.

'You might be,' she replied, 'you look familiar.'

What do toilets and anniversaries have in common?

Men always miss them.

'Does your husband play cards for money?'

'No, but the men he plays against do.'

'Did you hear about the stupid farmer who traded his only horse for a bale of hay?'

'What does he intend to do with the hay?'

'He's going to see if he can borrow back the horse long enough to get rid of it.'

'How did you meet your boyfriend?'

'I was crossing a street when this car drove up and stopped with a big jerk. It was him.'

How do we know that Adam was a stupid man?

Because he came first – they all do.

What does a man really mean when he says he's separated from his wife?

She's at home with the children, and I'm here, alone, with you.

**How can you tell if
a stupid man cooked dinner?**

The salad's burnt.

How are men like dogs?

*One stroke, and they follow
you everywhere.*

**Why is swapping partners
with your friend a bad mistake?**

*Because it's so depressing when
you get him back.*

**What do you call a man who
opens the car door for you?**

A chauffeur.

What happened when the stupid man telephoned the sex-chat line?

The girl said 'Not tonight. I've got earache.'

What do you call ten stupid men in a circle?

A dope ring.

Man:
**Do you want to come up
for a nightcap?**

Woman:
**Why, hasn't anyone ever had
sex with you sober?**

**Why do some men like tying
a woman to the bed?**

*Because otherwise they'd run
once they'd seen him.*

I hate men who...

break wind in bed

The stupid man was filling out a form. When he came to the question 'sex', there were two boxes marked 'M' and 'F'. After thinking for a moment he ticked both boxes and wrote, 'also on Wednesdays occasionally'.

At the end of the first act, the wife stopped her husband from leaving the theatre. 'Didn't you like the first act?' she asked.

'Oh, I liked it alright,' he said, 'but the programme says the second act takes place two weeks later.'

What's the difference between woman's bra size and a man's IQ?

Nothing, they're both the same.

Did you hear about the man who died at the height of passion?

He came and went at the same time.

The stupid man joined the police. On his first day he was given an intelligence test. The last question was: Who killed Jesus Christ?

'Great,' he thought, 'my first day and they expect me to solve a murder!'

Did you hear about the stupid Olympic skier who was so proud of his gold medal he had it bronzed?

Did you hear about the stupid kidnapper?

He enclosed a stamped, self-addressed envelope with the ransom note.

A man visits his doctor:
'Doctor, doctor, I haven't been
feeling myself today.'

'It's a good thing,' came the reply,
'that's an awful habit.'

'Did you know that all night long you were cursing me in my sleep?' said the husband to his wife.

'Who said I was sleeping?'

I hate men who...

practise imaginary golf swings

When the stupid man's grandfather died, he rang the local newspaper to print the death notice. 'That will be £25 per inch.' the clerk said.

'I can't afford that,' said the dope, 'he was six foot four.'

'Mrs Hardy, the court is going to
see to it that you receive £1,500
a month in alimony.'

'Thanks judge,' said Mr Hardy,
'I'll be sure to give her a
few bob myself.'

A wise person once said that a
woman is incomplete until she's
married... and then she's finished.

'I'm delighted with the doctor's physical, dear. He said I have the breasts of a woman half my age.'

'Yeah, but what did he say about your sixty-year-old ass?'

'Come to think of it, he didn't even mention your name.'

**Wife to her husband:
'Did you know that drinking
makes you handsome dear?'**

'But I don't drink.' he said, puzzled.

'No,' she smiled, 'but I do.'

**Did you hear about the guy who
rushed his pregnant wife to the pizza
parlour because he heard they
advertised free deliveries?**

'Mummy, what's a pauper?'

'Why that's another name for father, dear.'

Did you hear about the dumb guy who went to the luggage shop and asked for seven overnight cases?

He was going away for a week.

The stupid man's wife complained
that he was no use in bed so he
consulted his doctor.

'You're in terrible shape.' said the doc.
'Give up the booze and fags and run
ten miles a day. Your wife will
be amazed.'

Two weeks later he phoned the doctor
to tell him it worked, he was in
great shape.

'Is your wife amazed?' asked the doc.

'How would I know? I'm 150 miles
from home.'

A woman was complaining to
her friend: 'For two-and-a-half weeks
I didn't know where my husband was.
And then one night I went home –
and there he was.'

I hate men who...

swish plonk around their mouths

**How do you break
a dumb man's finger?**

Punch him in the nose.

MAN TO WOMAN, WOMAN TO MAN

Man:
**You're lucky we met. People like
me don't grow on trees.**

Woman:
No, they swing from them.

Man:
**I think I could make you
very happy.**

Woman:
Why – are you leaving?

Woman to man:
**Brains aren't everything,
but in your case they're nothing.**

Man:
I find you strangely appealing.
Woman:
I just find you strange.

**What do you call your husband when
he turns up with flowers?**
Guilty.

Man:
Have you had a wonderful evening?

Woman:
Sure, but it wasn't this one.

Man:
You know, nowadays a man can get rich and famous without having a brain in his head.

Woman:
You didn't.

Woman to man:
**Over eighty thousand sperm and
yours had to make it.**

DICTIONARY OF DOPES

**Definition of a stupid man:
one who, when you ask him how he is,
insists on telling you.**

**My boyfriend is so stupid, he thinks
fellatio is a character in *Hamlet*.**

**Did you hear about the man who
was so stupid he thought** *coq au vin*
was sex in a truck?

**My boyfriend's so stupid he
thinks** *genitalia* **is the name of
an Italian airline.**

The very stupid lay-man's glossary:

artery
the study of painting

fibula
a small lie

enema
not a friend

labour pain
getting hurt at work

nitrate
cheaper than day rate

Did you hear about the guy
who thinks *adage* is something
under-age boys do when they want
to go drinking down at the pub.

My boyfriend is so stupid he
thinks a *specimen* is an
Italian spaceman.

**What's the definition
of a *marriage*?**

A broken engagement.

**What's a stupid man's definition
of a *coquette*?**

A small soft drink.

**My boyfriend is so stupid he
thinks *impotent* means someone
who's well known.**

What's the difference between a pig and a stupid man?

There are some things even a pig wouldn't do!

My husband is so stupid he thinks a *mammogram* means the shiny pictures they're putting on credit cards these days.

MENtal breakdown
MENopause
MENstrual cramps
MENtal fatigue

...Ever notice how all our problems begin with MEN?

STUPID MEN QUIZ

Why are guys like public toilets?

1) They're engaged.

2) They're vacant.

3) They're full of crap.

How are men like UFOs?

1) You don't know where they're coming from.

2) You don't know what their mission is.

3) You don't know when they're going to take off.

Why is a stupid man like old age?

1) Neither has many advantages.

2) They both make women depressed.

3) They both come too soon.

Why does a stupid man like having two women in bed?

*1) So that he can come and
go at the same time.*

*2) So that he can see double without
having to buy a drink.*

*3) So that they have someone
to talk to.*

What is a stupid man's idea of safe sex?

1) Not doing it on top of scaffolding.

2) Doing it when his wife's away.

3) Giving you a false name and address.

Your man's idea of a balanced diet is:

1) Eating on one leg.

2) Leaving the crusts on his egg soldiers.

3) A six-pack in each hand.

When your man takes off his dirty clothes he will:

1) Smell them.

2) Drop them on the floor.

3) Watch them walk out of the door on their own.

Your man thinks he's a wonderful lover because:

1) He sends women into screaming fits.

2) He's faster than anyone else.

3) He practises a lot on his own.

What does your man remind you of?

1) How easy it is to make mistakes.

2) A headache you once had.

3) The last time you had exploratory surgery.

QUOTES

ON MEN, SEX,
LOVE AND MARRIAGE
AND
REALLY STUPID MEN

MEN

I require only three things of a man. He must be handsome, ruthless and stupid.

Dorothy Parker

My ancestors wandered lost in the wilderness for forty years because even in biblical times, men would not stop to ask for directions.

Elaine Boosler

Women want mediocre men, and men are working hard to become as mediocre as possible.

Margaret Mead

He's the type of man who will end up dying in his own arms.

Mamie Van Doren (on Warren Beatty)

My husband knows so much about rearing children that I've suggested he has the next one and I'll sit back and give advice.

The Princess of Wales

In politics, if you want anything said, ask a man; if you want anything done, ask a woman.

Margaret Thatcher

I like men who behave like men – strong and childish.

Francoise Sagan

Whatever women do they must do twice as hard as men to be thought half as good. Luckily, this is not difficult.

Charlotte Whitton

The people I'm furious with are the women's liberationists. They keep getting up on soap boxes and proclaiming that women are brighter than men. It's true but it should be kept quiet or it ruins the whole racket.

Anita Loos

The only time a woman really succeeds in changing a man is when he's a baby.

Natalie Wood

His mother should have thrown him away and kept the stork.

Mae West

**The more I see of men,
the more I like dogs.**

Germaine de Staël

**Women have many faults,
men have only two: everything they say,
and everything they do.**

Anonymous

This man has child-bearing lips.

Joan Rivers on Mick Jagger

**I'm the modern, intelligent type
of woman – in other words
I can't get a man.**

Shelley Winters

If Robert de Niro gains weight for a role it's called 'artistic dedication', if I do it's called letting yourself go.

Brenda Fricker

All men are rats – and those who aren't are boring.

Joan Collins

**I didn't leave him for another man...
but another woman – me.**

Cher

I leave before being left. I decide.

Brigitte Bardot

It is possible that blondes also prefer gentlemen.

Mamie Van Doren

Macho does not prove mucho.

Zsa Zsa Gabor

**The male is a domestic animal
which, if treated with firmness
and kindness, can be trained
to do most things.**

Jilly Cooper

**...perhaps men should
think twice before making
widowhood our only path
to power.**

Gloria Steinem

Why are women so much more interesting to men than men are to women?

Virginia Woolf

I never married because there was no need. I have three pets at home which answer the same purpose as a husband. I have a dog which growls every morning, a parrot which swears all the afternoon and a cat that comes home late at night.

Marie Corelli

**A woman without a man is like
a fish without a bicycle.**

Gloria Steinem

**Behind every woman you ever
heard of stands a man who
let her down.**

Naomi Bliven

SEX

**There's really nothing wrong
with a woman welcoming all men's
advances, as long as they are
in cash.**

Zsa Zsa Gabor

**I'm trying to get myself into shape
and she's the shape I'm trying
to get myself into.**

Anonymous

**Nothing happened in our marriage:
I named the waterbed Lake Placid.**

Phyllis Diller

Middle age is the time of life when a man's fantasies revolve around a bank manager saying 'yes' instead of a girl.

Jane Fonda

A woman can have twenty-five affairs and nobody says anything, but if she has four husbands she's terrible.

Hedy Lamarr

My doctor told my wife that we should enjoy sex every night – now we never see each other.

Chevy Chase

I feel like a million tonight – but one at a time please.

Mae West

All discarded lovers should be given a second chance, but with somebody else.

Mae West

Never trust a husband too far, nor a bachelor too near.

Helen Rowland

**The average man is more interested
in a woman who is interested
in him than he is in a woman with
beautiful legs.**

Marlene Dietrich

**Some men are all right in their place –
if they only knew the right places!**

Mae West

I am happy now that Charles calls on my bed chamber less frequently of old. As it is I now endure but two calls a week and when I hear his steps outside my door I lie down on my bed, close my eyes, open my legs and think of England.

Lady Alice Hillington, 1912

Unless there's some emotional tie, I'd rather play tennis.

Bianca Jagger

In my sex fantasy, nobody ever loves me for my mind.

Nora Ephron

Is that a gun in your pocket, or are you just glad to see me?

Mae West

LOVE AND MARRIAGE

**Never go to bed mad.
Stay up and fight.**

Phyllis Diller

Whenever you want to marry someone, go have lunch with his ex-wife.

Shelley Winters

There is nothing worse than solitude, growing old without a shoulder to lean on. Marry, marry – even if he's fat and boring!

Coco Chanel

The majority of husbands remind me of an orang-utan trying to play the violin.

Balzac

The husband who wants a happy marriage should learn to keep his mouth shut and his cheque book open.

Groucho Marx

Marriage is a great institution, but I'm not ready for an institution.

Mae West

The reason that husbands and wives do not understand each other is because they belong to different sexes.

Dorothy Dix

**I'm not sure if I'm staying married
for love or spite.**

Anonymous

**All I ever got from Hollywood was
three lousy ex-husbands.**

Ava Gardner

It's bloody impractical to love, honour and obey. If it wasn't, you wouldn't have to sign a contract.

Katherine Hepburn

Asked if she believed in large families, Zsa Zsa Gabor replied, 'Oh yes – every woman should have three husbands.'

Asked who she was going to marry next, Zsa Zsa Gabor replied, 'A man who appreciates the finer things in life – diamonds, furs... and me.'

I married a few people I shouldn't have, but haven't we all?

Mamie Van Doren

The surest way to be alone is to get married.

Gloria Steinem

When a girl gets married she exchanges the attention of many men for the inattention of one.

Helen Rowland

My husband said he wanted to have a relationship with a redhead, so I dyed my hair red.

Jane Fonda

REALLY STUPID MEN

**What was Watergate?
A little bugging!**

Richard Nixon

**I called the doctor and
he told me the contraptions
were an hour apart.**

*Mackey Sasser,
New York Mets Catcher, on his wife's labour*

**Everyone who is for abortion was
at one time a faeces.**

*Peter Grace, in an introduction
to a Ronald Reagan speech*

**I've just returned from
10 Drowning Street so I know
what I'm talking about.**

Samuel Goldwyn in a political argument

**What a waste to lose one's mind –
or not to have a mind.
How true that is.**

*Vice President Dan Quayle garbling a
United Negro College Fund slogan
'a mind is a terrible thing to waste'*

They pushed their nomination down my throat behind my back.

J. Ramsay MacDonald, then MP, modestly denying any role in the honour he was about to receive.

So Carol, you're a housewife and mother. And have you got any children?

Michael Barrymore